The Future of
VIDEO GAMING

Tom Streissguth

ReferencePoint Press
San Diego, CA

ReferencePoint Press®

Printed in the United States

For more information, contact:
ReferencePoint Press, Inc.
PO Box 27779
San Diego, CA 92198
www.ReferencePointPress.com

LIBRARY OF CONGRESS CATALOGING-IN-PUBLICATION DATA

Name: Streissguth, Tom- author
Title: The Future of Video Gaming/by Tom Streissguth
Description: San Diego, CA: ReferencePoint Press, Inc, 2027. |
Includes bibliographical references and index.
Identifiers: LCCN 2026013141 (print) | ISBN
9781678213404 library binding | ISBN 9781678213411 ebook
Subjects: LCSH: Juvenile literature

For compete cataloging-in-publication data please go to www.loc.gov.

CONTENTS

Strange New Games

Since the days of early arcade games such as *Pong* and *Space Invaders*, the video game industry has been growing fast, reaching new gamers and new markets worldwide. Games jumped to personal computers in the 1980s, then to consoles such as PlayStation and Xbox, and then to the internet. Developers came up with new genres such as real-time strategy games and first-person shooters. Massively multiplayer online games built big communities of players engaged in epic battles and the creation of alternative worlds in the metaverse.

It is a moneymaking enterprise. "Within the United States, video games generated an annual revenue of nearly $100 billion," according to a 2023 report by the tech industry analysts at Contrary Research, "while globally the industry rakes in more than twice as much. This makes the global gaming industry five times bigger than Hollywood, bigger than the film and music industries combined."[1]

> **"The global gaming industry [is] five times bigger than Hollywood, bigger than the film and music industries combined."[1]**
>
> —Contrary Research, tech industry analysis company

The huge revenues of the industry feed the development of new capabilities that make video games constantly more distinctive and creative. Faster processors and high-rendering graphics cards, for example, make visual details realistic and gameplay more exciting. Newer computers, gaming consoles, and online servers reach the market every year, allowing players to enjoy the next generation of games.

New Possibilities

The future holds fascinating new possibilities, with the speed of innovation making it difficult for many gamers to keep up and leaving them unaware of the amazing new tech that is reaching the market. Virtual reality (VR) projectors, for example, are building 3-D holographic worlds. Augmented reality allows imaginary objects to interact with the real world. Instead of keyboards and controllers, games are operating on voice commands. Haptic gear is now allowing players to feel physical sensations rendered by the game, such as a punch, a rain shower, or a slight breath of wind. With neural links, a gamer can even control gameplay hands-free—with their thoughts. Predicting the possible future of gaming, Tencent Cloud, an internet and computing support service, imagines a gaming experience in which players can shape more aspects of gameplay. The site suggests that with speech recognition, for example, "VR storytelling could become more interactive if users can influence the plot through dialogue."[2]

The future also holds excitement in the use of non-player characters (NPCs) or companions. These NPCs have always been a big part of the fun. In the past, they could be quite predictable, responding to a few dialogue options, with their actions determined by logic trees and programming code. But as the artificial intelligence (AI) voice engine Inworld asks, "What if games did things differently and allowed players to interact with NPCs unscripted? What if you could play with NPCs that could respond to absolutely anything you asked them—in real-time?"[3]

The NPC built on this new unscripted model may invite a player to time travel to another place or time. By integrating the player's social media history, it may come up with a favorite location and integrate photographs and videos the player has already taken. It would move in unexpected ways, reacting to the player's own commands.

Gaming's New AI Dimensions

One key development in computer science that is already changing the gaming landscape is artificial intelligence. AI means training computers to imitate human thought, and with generative AI, human creation. It promises to turn the static, passive experience of playing a game into something entirely different: a process in which the player becomes the developer and the game is different for everyone who logs on and hits the start button.

AI is already at work in games like *No Man's Sky*. There, generative AI programming allows for this interstellar exploration simulator to map an entire universe of planets with procedurally generated biomes and inhabitants that make each feel slightly novel. Designers believe AI could eventually allow characters, plotlines, and environments to become dynamic in future games, giving players an individualized experience during each playthrough.

In just a few decades, video games have become the biggest entertainment industry on the planet, holding a place in popular culture alongside television, sports, and movies. They also at-

Huge industry revenues feed the development of new capabilities for video games. Ever faster processors make visual details realistic and gameplay more exciting.

tract the attention of tech philosophers and futurists, who enjoy speculating on how games will amaze players in the decades to come. There are fascinating changes to come, from generative AI to neural interfaces to new genres that go beyond traditional role-playing games and first-person shooters. Although they work in keen competition with each other, developers always strive to bring cutting edge tech to the field. With the many new experiences coming to this medium and the new gaming challenges to overcome, players will experience games that reflect their interests and play styles and make them active participants in game creation.

CHAPTER ONE

The Backstory

The first video games were created in computer research labs. In 1958 William Higinbotham programmed *Tennis for Two*, which could be played on an oscilloscope, a device to measure electronic voltage by examining corresponding wave shapes on a small screen. In the 1960s at the Massachusetts Institute of Technology, Steve Russell built *Spacewar!*, a space combat simulation, to be played on a refrigerator-sized computer. Higinbotham and Russell designed these programs as light entertainments. They did not think of their computer games as commercial products. There were no home computers, and pinball was the only electronic game in arcades or other public spaces.

That changed in 1972, when the American company Atari released *Pong*. It was like a game of Ping-Pong or tennis, with two players batting a small dot back and forth across a screen. *Pong* appeared in bars and eventually in video arcades, where players fed quarters into a big wooden cabinet with a video screen. Other games—like *Space Invaders*, *Pac-Man*, *Donkey Kong*, and *Asteroids*—also became big hits during the arcade boom in the late 1970s and early 1980s. To bring the games into consumers' homes, Atari came out with a small console that could be plugged into a television. Beginning in 1977, *Pong* and other games were released on small plastic cartridges operated by the console.

Video games migrated to personal computers (PCs) in the 1980s. The PC was something new in the home. It offered the processing power of the refrigerator-sized computers in a small box with a screen. Because PCs were still seen primarily as business tools, video game consoles remained the more popular option for most gamers. In 1994 Sony introduced the first PlayStation console. Two years later, the Nintendo 64 appeared. Improved graphics cards began expanding color options and creating sharper details, making games more immersive. Game graphics went 3-D in the early 1990s with titles like *Wolfenstein 3D* and *Doom*. Racing games, fighting games, dungeon crawlers, and platformers took advantage of the new graphics and faster processing speeds. Real-time strategy games and role-playing games offered massive maps, interactive NPCs, and intricate storylines that played out like epic feature films.

PlayStation went through several new generations and in 2000 gained a tough competitor: Microsoft's Xbox. As the processing power of consoles and personal computers improved, games became more realistic—and harder to beat. Dedicated players did not mind the challenges of these new games. Instead, they relished their hard-fought victories and looked forward to even tougher games. Their enthusiasm and loyalty drove revenues of the video game industry in the United States alone to over $11 billion in 2002.

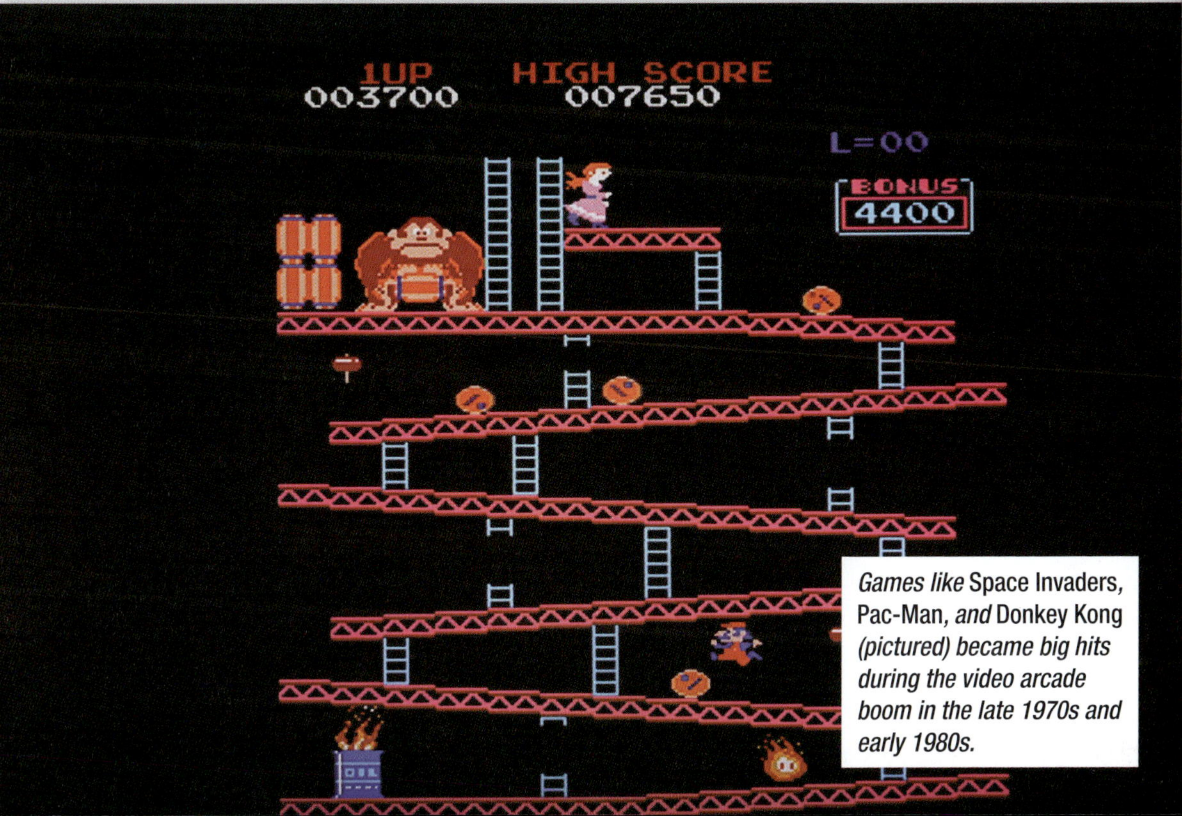

Games like Space Invaders, Pac-Man, *and* Donkey Kong *(pictured) became big hits during the video arcade boom in the late 1970s and early 1980s.*

New Game Tech

From the mid-1990s through the early 2000s, online gaming ushered in the next evolution in video game playing. Multiplayer mode on PCs allowed gamers to join others for role-playing adventures such as *Final Fantasy* and *Baldur's Gate*. In 2000 Sony joined this trend with the PlayStation 2, which supported online gaming. The company soon had competition in the online space with Microsoft's Xbox Live and a handful of titles offered by Nintendo's GameCube.

Young gamers of the prior generation were growing older. Many of them were introduced to the tech industries through gaming. They considered coding a game to be one of life's greatest challenges, and their skill at gaming became a point of pride. Mark Zuckerberg, who was born in 1984 and is the cofounder and chief executive officer (CEO) of Facebook, has been playing *Civilization* for a very long time. "I think at some point, I should do like a Twitch stream of me playing with someone," he once told a reporter. "Because I'm pretty convinced that I'm close to grandmaster status. I'd be surprised if anyone in the world could beat me at that."[4]

> **"I'm pretty convinced that I'm close to grandmaster status. I'd be surprised if anyone in the world could beat me at [*Civilization*]."[4]**
>
> —Mark Zuckerberg, cofounder and chief executive officer of Facebook

In the early 2000s, faster processors in consoles and PCs continued to shape graphics and gameplay, opening new possibilities. Virtual reality gaming arrived in 2016 with headsets such as the Oculus and HTC Vive. VR tech made it possible to experience a game in a unique way. Instead of viewing a flat screen, gamers were immersed in a 3-D space. They could navigate a house, dungeon, or forest with 360-degree vision; hear spatialized sounds from any direction; and grab, aim, or manipulate objects with physical controllers.

Games were also getting smarter. Developers strived to improve the game's reaction to the player's moves and playing style—a design aspect known in this field as artificial intelligence. Better AI meant a more challenging game, one in which computer opponents reacted more logically to players' actions. This type

Bridging Games, Television, and Movies

In the twenty-first century, several video game franchises were turned into cable programs and movies. Cable shows such as *The Last of Us* and *Fallout* were adapted from popular games, and films based on *Sonic* and *Five Nights at Freddy's* characters and narratives screened in theaters. Producers see no end to the trend, given the success of many similar projects.

In the future, TV, movies, and video games might merge into a new genre altogether. The first interactive television show was *Black Mirror: Bandersnatch*, which allowed viewers to direct the plot with a series of simple choices on their viewing device. Depending on the choices made, each viewer could reach one of five distinct endings to the story.

The development of a single story across multiple platforms is known as a transmedia narrative. "Interactive features like quizzes, challenges, and companion apps help in deeper involvement and encourage repeat viewings," states the game news and review website PSX Extreme. "For example, Netflix's *Stranger Things* collaborated with mobile games to extend its narrative universe, making a cohesive transmedia experience." Bringing together film or television with video games is creating a new medium in which viewers become players and the platforms offer new opportunities to extend storylines across different media experiences.

PSX Extreme, "The Intersection of Online Gaming and Movies/TV Shows," February 20, 2025. https://psxextreme.com.

of AI, however, relied on predetermined, coded responses, and its patterns could be learned by observant gamers. Its "thinking" was not yet adaptive and dynamic.

Looking to the Future

Gamers have always looked forward to more realistic environments, smarter in-game opponents, and other advances in game technology. Games like *Grand Theft Auto*, *Final Fantasy*, and *Assassin's Creed* yielded a long series of sequels and new editions, each offering something new in gameplay and graphics. Competitive gaming offered tournaments and sponsorships to the world's best gamers. Fans could go to online streaming channels such as Twitch to watch the real experts play.

In 2017 the battle royale game *Fortnite* quickly became an international smash hit. Players signed up to compete against a huge online community that grew year after year. The game was free to play, while in-game purchases and upgrades earned the publisher Epic Games almost $6 billion in 2024 alone. Game developers invested enormous sums in these franchises, feeding a market hungry for new and better gaming experiences.

Virtual reality continued to offer gamers new experiences. While the early headsets and controllers were tethered to computers, newer models, like the Meta Quest series, are standalone, allowing players much freer movement. Graphics have also improved, creating more impressive visual details, lighting, and natural motion.

In augmented reality (AR), a cousin to virtual reality, game settings and assets are projected onto the real world. *Pokémon GO*, in which players hunt and train mythical animals from the *Pokémon* universe, was the first popular AR game, arriving in 2016. Extended reality, or XR, glasses make it possible to project an augmented reality game directly onto a lens worn over the eyes, making headsets and traditional screens unnecessary. An Android XR platform launched in 2025.

Pokémon GO *(pictured), in which players hunt and train mythical animals from the Pokémon universe, was the first popular AR game, arriving in 2016.*

New Systems and New Genres

By 2026 the ninth generation of gaming systems had arrived. PlayStation brought out the PS5 in 2020, and Microsoft's Xbox Series X debuted the same year. The Xbox Galaxy Black Special Edition was reengineered with the fastest game processor on the market and one or two terabytes of storage in 2024. Personal computers designed for gaming can more quickly take advantage of the latest processing and graphics technology, since they can be updated more often than consoles. These PCs, however, are costly to build or purchase.

In contrast to televisions and other consumer electronics, gaming systems—and the games themselves—were getting more expensive. To beef up their revenue streams and lessen the sticker shock of high game prices at retail stores, major developers came up with monthly subscriptions to access game libraries. These companies also earned money from in-game purchases, such as better weapons and new "skins" (clothing) for game avatars. In addition to large-scale studio products, a new sector of this industry took off. Mobile games could be designed by anyone with coding skills and a clever idea. These games were cheap to download, easy to learn, and available to anybody with an iPhone or an Android device. This ensured their rapid growth through the 2020s.

Mobile games inspired creators to branch out into new looks and gameplay styles. Video gaming had a long history of familiar subject matter: first-person shooters, role-playing, sports, racing, horror, and platformers. Most gamers appreciated the familiarity of these genres, but they were also eagerly looking for new offerings. Mobile titles included puzzles, word games, and other social activities that could draw in new, diverse audiences, not merely die-hard veterans.

AI on the Horizon

Around 2022 more dynamic artificial intelligence burst on the tech scene and wove its way into game design and gameplay.

This was something different from the rule-based, often predictable AI of early video games. Since that era, several companies—including OpenAI, Anthropic, Microsoft, and Google—had been training computers on data "scraped" from the internet. Coupled with more complex algorithms, this training allowed computer applications to imitate the logic and processing abilities of the human brain. AI chatbots could now answer questions posed by users and seem quite human while doing so. Generative AI, like ChatGPT, could write stories, movie scripts, and music. For many people in the gaming industries, this breakthrough seemed to threaten jobs. For others, it promised another creative outlet.

Most video game companies eagerly adopted the new technology. Powerful AI tools, in video games and many other creative fields, generated "original" work, even if it was based on the AI's study of existing human-made text and images. These tools also cut back on the time-consuming routine tasks involved in creating a video game. No longer would game developers need to spend months and years writing and testing programming code. AI could write and test code very quickly. With existing code or gaming engines, AI could also model terrain and character movement more realistically, and in a much shorter time than human developers could.

> **"During the first two months of 2024, there have already been some 8,000 job losses [in the video game industry]."[5]**
>
> —Matthew Ball, video game industry analyst

AI capabilities, however, led to the elimination of many jobs in the video game industry, especially for entry-level programmers, designers, and artists. "In 2022, the industry had a then-record of 8,500 layoffs," says industry analyst Matthew Ball in a web article. "2023 beat that record by nearly 25%. And during the first two months of 2024, there have already been some 8,000 job losses."[5] Many companies state that such job displacement is part of a larger industry correction, but a 2025 survey by the Game Developers Conference also noted that 30 percent of respondents from the field believe AI is having a detrimental effect on game quality and design.

Making Work into a Game

Gamification is a term that means turning work, school, or business, into a game-like process. It is done to keep people interested and engaged in areas of life not traditionally associated with fun. The popularity of gamification has spread because several generations of students and workers are very familiar with video games.

Medicine is one field that is gamifying tasks. Medical games can train health care workers, for example, by presenting a menu of options of care for a specific injury or disease. The games guide the player to the best process to treat a patient's illness or concern. Similarly, health and wellness games offer exercise routines, diet choices, and lifestyle changes so players feel better and can keep from experiencing medical problems.

Many different game platforms are available for kids and adults with attention-deficit/hyperactivity disorder. Play Attention is one of these game systems that uses biofeedback. The user wears an armband that measures concentration. While gaming, the attention signal manipulates the mouse, cursor, or joystick of the game on a video screen. The game encourages players to ignore distractions, complete missions or tasks, and focus.

These gaming elements within traditional types of medical prevention and care are helping providers and patients manage illnesses and disorders.

The Metaverse and a New Web

Despite the industry's growing fears, AI was enabling small-group or individual game designers to build their own worlds. By prompting AI tools to generate game characters, dialogue, user interfaces, and other assets, even players could create games and make them as easy or challenging as they liked. Generative AI technology continues to promise to make game design accessible to a much wider audience.

Gamers were also eagerly adopting the immersive worlds of the metaverse. A metaverse is an online or digital world, complete with its own geography, culture, economy, and social interactions among users. Among the most popular in the 2020s were those associated with *Minecraft*, *Roblox*, *Star Atlas*, and *The Sandbox*. These environments challenge players to do much more than defeat opponents or get to a final boss battle. Users can assume a new personality with avatars they create, and these avatars can build, trade, and socialize with few limitations.

A metaverse is an online or digital world. Minecraft *was one of the most popular metaverse games in the 2020s.*

Along with metaverse gaming arose the new platforms of Web3 technology. Web3 is all about users taking personal control of the internet so that they will no longer depend on huge technology companies who gather their data and use social media and other platforms to market consumer goods. For gamers, Web3 allows players to buy, sell, and trade assets through a secure system of ownership known as the blockchain. Instead of "renting" powerful in-game items, skins, or characters from developers, users will own these assets and can sell them to other individuals through an exchange of cryptocurrency. Through the blockchain, gaming offers a means for players to make money by completing difficult challenges, acquiring rare items, and building high-tier inventories. By enabling a player-driven marketplace, Web3 gaming promotes deeper engagement and long-term participation on the part of players, benefiting gamers as well as developers.

New and Future Genres

With new technology and new platforms, game genres will expand. While many traditional games focus on overcoming challenges, confronting opponents, and solving puzzles, newer offerings include playing or creating together in a shared world, combining gameplay with real-world activities like learning a language or running a business. Sandbox games, such as *Light No Fire* and *Crimson Desert*, provide a setting, such as a city or an entire planet, in which players can build their own environments. An "idle" game encourages players to build and upgrade the processes that gather resources and turn them into products for in-game currency. The goal is to streamline the processes and let the game run itself even when the player is not interacting with it.

Video games have become the world's most popular and profitable entertainment medium, and new technology will bring in new players with interests that go beyond what previous games could satisfy. Once targeted to teenagers, video games now engage older audiences. Gaming tech will move into new sectors such as schools, businesses, and communications, and daily life for many people will be spent among an online community created and managed by a game. The future possibilities for the medium are limited only by human imagination.

The Influence of AI

AI in video games goes all the way back to *Pac-Man*. This 1980s arcade game set the player dashing through a maze while trying to evade four hungry ghosts. *Pac-Man* had 256 levels and was very tough to beat. The game seemed to think fast and make the right decisions on where to send Blinky, Pinky, Inky and Clyde, its non-player characters. As defeated players fished out another quarter to try again, they wondered how those little ghosts got so smart.

Ever since *Pac-Man* cabinets showed up in restaurants, shopping malls, and game arcades, artificial intelligence has been a trendy concept in video games. It helped game programmers make their games challenging. A game with "good AI" was able to make its NPCs more skillful, clever, and dangerous. As *Pac-Man* demonstrated, the ability to respond to the player's actions was part of a video game's attraction.

While early video game AI followed programmed rules and predictable patterns, modern AI mirrors real-time decision-making and human reasoning. ChatGPT, for example, answers questions and writes coherent essays in response to a user prompt. DALL-E is an image generator that also creates visual art based on a user's written description. These and other programs can write music, analyze medical tests, and handle video editing.

Programmers accomplished this by feeding computer systems a massive amount of data and training them to find patterns within. Provided with enough data, it is possible for machines to discover the most used and accepted patterns and then hold a dialogue, generate an original text, or even create a video game that mirrors those patterns. For example, ChatGPT can generate essays because it has learned patterns across billions of books, articles, and other texts in its training data.

Game Building

Game developers are taking advantage of generative AI to build games more efficiently. Promethean AI, for example, is a game design tool that can build worlds and objects in a consistent style. From a detailed prompt provided by a human developer, Promethean AI creates characters, objects, and environments rapidly, saving designers the time needed for 3-D modeling. If a designer asks the AI tool to create the interior of a fantasy tavern, the program builds an image of the tables, chairs, lighting, and characters commonly found in such settings based on its training data.

Beyond imagery, AI can also assist designers in conveying realistic motion. To portray walking, running, jumping, or flying, programmers normally must use code to move 3-D digital models to

Modern video game AI mirrors real-time decision-making and human reasoning. DALL-E (pictured) is an AI image generator that also creates visual art based on a user's written description.

imitate the appropriate actions. This task has grown easier with AI software such as Cascadeur. This software uses algorithms that analyze the size and shape of a moving object as a series of static frames. Replicating the physics of movement patterns it has studied, the AI then inserts AI-generated frames between artist-created frames to make the motion of that object fluid, stiff, hyperrealistic, or dreamlike, as the designer wishes. Some AI tools allow designers to turn two-dimensional drawings into 3-D characters or fashion natural movements from text prompts.

For game publishers, AI has become a powerful tool that saves time and money. A game publisher, or even a solo creator, can assign routine coding and the design of interfaces, menus, and cutscenes to artificial intelligence. If the developer needs to fill out dialogue, find plot holes in a story, or devise music cues, generative AI can make logical suggestions. AI tools can also streamline the huge task of debugging code, which in the past might take hundreds of hours of work by programmers.

"This technology can also be used to test games during development," explains the AI website Globant, "providing feedback and identifying issues by simulating countless playthroughs at a speed no human tester could achieve."[6] Human game testers play through a game to check that it plays well. They also try to "break" the game by performing actions that are counterintuitive but possible. Errors are recorded and bugs are fixed, and then the testers play through again to find more errors and inconsistencies.

In the past, this process took a lot of time. AI can run through a game millions of times in a relatively short period, finding errors and even logging plot elements that might be too difficult or boring for many players. This saves creators time and money, allowing cleaner and more engaging video games.

Marketing Games

AI systems are also being deployed to market and sell games. For instance, game publishers deploy predictive AI, which uses detailed sales data to figure out which genres are most popular. AI can also analyze churn, the percentage of players who stop playing a game after a short time. AI also relies on event logs that are generated by in-game events, such as logging in, quitting, switching characters, choosing new weapons, or picking out skins. Servers send the information to a data warehouse, where a machine learning platform applies analytical tools to the data. As one example, Riot Games, which produces *League of Legends*, found that players who played the game alone were more likely to quit. The company built a "friend activity nudge" to get solo players into group sessions and introduced new content at levels where churn was more likely.

In the future, the data gathered by AI tools will become more central in the player experience as well. AI will measure how much time players spend on certain levels or quests, and the choices they are making in a multiplayer setting. This data will feed the AI models that adjust the non-player characters, skins, and weapons according to player preferences—subtly building in motivations to stay with a game longer. AI can also act as a matchmaker

Riot Games, which produces League of Legends, *designed a method to get solo players into group sessions and introduced new content at higher levels to maintain player commitment.*

for opponents in the online multiplayer format, as in *Fortnite*, so that players feel more challenged and might persevere because of the social aspect of the game.

The Personalized Game

AI will also be able to draw on the data it collects on each player to "personalize" the game experience. Video games already provide players with some limited options that can change gameplay over various playthroughs. For example, when interacting with NPCs, players might be given a choice of text prompts that will influence the outcome of the encounter. Choosing one response might convince an NPC to reveal the location of a treasure, while another selection might turn the character hostile. This will change the resulting gameplay in that playthrough.

AI promises to expand such interactions, allowing developers to make NPCs more human and realistic. Inworld makes software used by game designers to build what are known as advanced NPCs. The Inworld character engine works through a library of templates. These help developers model non-player characters

Dueling and Dealing with AI

In future gaming, AI bots may take their places as in-game opponents. A human player who has achieved a high score or level in a game can make another playthrough more interesting by setting up a role for an AI program. For example, a big part of the challenge in the new "social deduction" genre is identifying who in the game is human and who is not. Using AI agents in such games might make the playthrough more difficult as artificial intelligence seeks to demonstrate its humanness.

Not all AI impacts on video games are expected to be positive. Gaming consultant Allen Chi writes that AI "makes it a challenge for developers to predict and control every aspect of the game. This lack of control can sometimes detract from the intended gaming experience, with the AI behaving in ways that weren't originally intended by the creators."

There also may be problems with computer memory and processing. AI tools "demand more from the game engine," explains Chi. Integrating AI in games may lead to more technical problems, such as software bugs, faulty gameplay, or crashes.

Allen Chi, "The Problem with AI in Gaming," Allen Chi personal website, October 16, 2023. https://allenchi.org.

with distinct personalities that respond to player actions with a greater and more realistic range of emotions. Many will remember how a character has behaved toward them in the past and act accordingly upon a future meeting. Some will retain the knowledge of old dialogues and work those topics into new encounters.

> "Imagine being able to walk into a world and have a truly believable conversation with a character."[7]
>
> —Phil Harrison, former vice president at Google

Phil Harrison, a gaming executive at Google, believes this will make gamers more aware of how they interact with NPCs, making each game a truly novel experience. "Imagine being able to walk into a world and have a truly believable conversation with a character," he told one interviewer, "where it feels like you're talking to a real human being. I think it will allow games to reach a new level of creativity, have even more richness and depth, creating a new medium beyond just the playing of games."[7]

Beyond NPC interactions, AI will begin to learn more about how each player chooses to operate within a gaming world. A game will know what kind of challenges gamers prefer, what attacks they are good at, or whether they like solving puzzles or role-playing. This data will prompt the game to change dynamically in response to gamers' preferences and play styles. "Games that can adapt themselves to you and produce a new, interesting world that it *knows* is interesting to you . . . that's going to come," says Julian Togelius, a computer science professor. "But it can also go too far. Some people would think it's extremely creepy."[8]

Player-Made Games

Personalizing playthroughs with AI in existing games may offer one kind of novelty, but AI also promises to allow gamers to build and play their own games. No programming skills will be necessary, and the expensive process of producing a game will become a task that anyone with basic computer skills can manage. To spin up one of these DIY games, generative AI simply incorporates user prompts into a template or interface.

Seele is one of these interface platforms, billing itself as the "leading no-code AI game maker." On the company's home page, Seele gives several examples of games created by the simple prompts of its users. One example in the restaurant management genre reads: "Create a 2D animal restaurant mini-game with a hand-drawn picture book art style. Players can click the 'Promote' button in the bottom right corner to attract various cute animals to the restaurant."[9]

Text-based adventures have become another important genre of AI-generated games. *AI Dungeon*, *Private Detective*, and *Origins* are role-playing games in which the player navigates levels, puzzles, and challenges and converses with AI non-player characters to reach a goal or solve a mystery. In these games, users follow an AI-generated narrative and then type in the actions they want to take in key situations. Some allow the players to take over the story at points, forcing the AI to adapt to the changes as the tale continues.

Google, which started as a search engine company, has taken on the challenge of creating interactive 3-D environments through

Collecting Data, Marketing to Segments

As the model for video games changed in the 2010s, game makers faced a new problem. Instead of charging for games up front, developers now adopted the free-to-play model. Games cost nothing to download, but players made additional purchases while playing. This meant games needed to keep players playing as long as possible. AI became an important tool in this effort.

To do this, AI helped companies segment their players. Data was collected on how often players played, how long they played each time, their style of play, and the history of their purchases. Each player was profiled with information on age, gender, buying habits, and interaction with other players. The players were grouped into segments according to their behavior patterns. The marketing department then targeted segments with ads designed for their members.

This segmentation is done in real time, as the players are playing. If players change how they play or buy, they are placed in a different segment. They will see new ads or game assets, timed differently, until they change their segment again. In the future, this strategy will become hyper-personalized so that individual players will see ads, trailers, gameplay, levels of violence, and other aspects of a game tailored just for them.

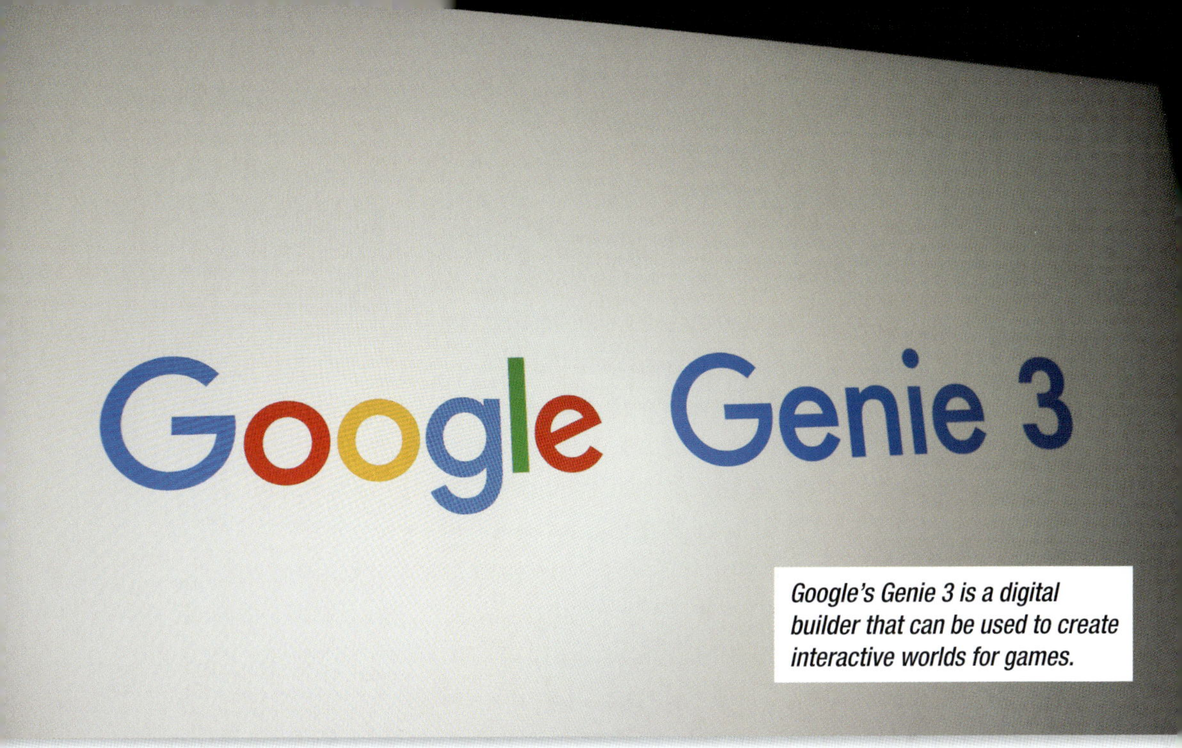

Google's Genie 3 is a digital builder that can be used to create interactive worlds for games.

AI prompts. In January 2026 the company released a new AI technology called Genie 3. This software is a digital builder, which creates worlds that are limited only by the imagination of the user.

In theory, with Genie 3, an entire game might be constructed in the future without any kind of template or supporting code. The user perspective can be set to first person, third person, or isometric. The lighting and physics of the world stay consistent, no matter the angle. The environments react to the mouse or keyboard, making it possible to walk, run, and explore. In the future, when Genie 3 becomes fully interactive, there may be no need for a video game designer to program, test, or use a game engine such as Unity as a starting point.

Dangers of AI Slop

But as in music, movies, and original writing, video game designers face the problem of "AI slop." This is mediocre, unimaginative content generated by AI models. AI slop arises from the fact that generative AI is trained on the works of the past and is not very good at breaking new ground in story, gameplay, or imagery. It simply lacks the stamp of human imagination and creativity.

"Many of this year's biggest games have faced backlash for GenAI usage."[10]

—Austin Gallagher, blogger

"Many of this year's biggest games have faced backlash for GenAI usage," reports blogger Austin Gallagher on the Medium site. "Audiences, especially gamers, seem poised to revolt against the pervasive push to replace human work with AI slop. Games that have been found to feature GenAI and lack disclosure have had to issue apologies."[10] Game developers of the future will be dealing with the AI slop issue until the models can—if ever—produce works of true originality.

"Every new technology comes with a fear of people being displaced and replaced, all the way back to the printing press."[11]

—Chris Hewish, president of Xsolla

AI's efficiencies raise other concerns in the industry. If the time-consuming process of designing and coding games can be turned over to AI software, the number of jobs requiring these skills will fall, and trained individuals may have to seek another line of work. "Every new technology comes with a fear of people being displaced and replaced, all the way back to the printing press," says Chris Hewish, an executive at the game commerce company Xsolla. He adds, though, "I think we'll have opportunities for creators who are versed in prompts with AI—who can actually work with AI as a partner."[11] This suggests that, like other industries, employees may need to adapt to the new technologies to remain competitive in a changing marketplace.

Entering Extended Reality

For many years, virtual reality was just an idea. A VR game, in theory, would put the player inside 3-D environments projected onto a screen. Ivan Sutherland, a computer researcher, saw the possibilities back in 1965. Imagining a computer-controlled simulation space with screens all around, he speculated, "There is no reason why the objects displayed by a computer have to follow the ordinary rules of physical reality. . . . The ultimate display would, of course, be a room within which the computer can control the existence of matter."[12]

> "There is no reason why the objects displayed by a computer have to follow the ordinary rules of physical reality."[12]
>
> —Ivan Sutherland, pioneering computer scientist

In the 2010s, technology began to catch up with the concept. Game and tech companies joined the drive to put out the first commercial VR gear. Instead of building 3-D chambers, virtual reality pioneers have adapted screens, headsets, special goggles, or even a simple pair of glasses to allow users to engage with a VR world wherever they like. Meta, PlayStation, Valve, Samsung, Sony, and Apple devised VR headsets. But these products did not always work well. Initially, the headsets were bulky and awkward, and until the release of the Samsung Gear VR in 2015, VR sets were tethered to computers and consoles by cables that limited free motion. The games themselves also had glitches and bugs. Wearing a VR headset could be disorienting and give the player an uncomfortable sense of isolation. Some players experienced nausea or dizziness.

For a few years, only a few playable VR games reached the market. Gradually, manufacturers developed better optical technology that made the simulated environments more realistic and the games more playable. Faster processors delivered more depth and realistic color to the screen. When stand-alone headsets hit the market, gamers had more freedom of movement. This change was a significant improvement for exercise games and VR sports such as tennis and golf.

Playing Games with the Real World

Augmented reality followed the VR revolution. AR places computer-generated objects and graphics atop the physical world. AR objects are visible through a phone screen, a headset, or specialized AR glasses. *Pokémon GO*, which came out in 2016, was the first AR game. It incorporated Global Positioning System data that used the player's real-world location. Players wandered through streets and parks to discover hidden *Pokémon* characters that the game placed on their maps and made visible through their phone cameras. AR had made it possible to get out of the house and play a digital game in the real world.

Through the 2020s, mobile AR went through upgrades and technical improvements. One of the most important is lidar, a system that uses a beam of laser light to precisely map the surroundings. Lidar offers better integration of AR objects into a game environment. Lidar-equipped glasses or mobile phones, for example, can place and hide objects realistically, making a virtual character appear on a sidewalk instead of floating a few feet above it.

New AR casual and puzzle games have followed the trend. *Angry Birds AR: Isle of Pigs*, for example, brought back one of the most popular casual games ever made. In the AR version, the player launches birds at 3-D objects, behind which pigs are hiding. Instead of seeing digital things projected on the phone, the user projects the entire game through the phone's camera, making it possible to turn a wall or a living room into the screen. The game's environment depends on where the user points the phone.

Gaming and tech companies have adapted headsets to allow users to engage with a VR world wherever they like.

Zombies, Run! applies a survival horror premise to an AR exercise game. The player sets duration or distance, chooses music, and then jogs, walks, or runs through a zombie apocalypse. The player can gather collectibles and supplies along the way. Some players use the app to train for real-world challenges such as 5K runs. The game also offers missions, with street maps of the player's location appearing on the phone to show the route.

Using an Android or iPhone as a platform gives AR a big advantage over VR, because just about everybody owns a mobile phone. In the future, AR games will be easy to play and easy to access. Web-based AR allows players to fire up an AR game simply by scanning a QR code on a website. That means no app downloads to the phone will be necessary. Some gamers will get into an AR session by simply putting on a pair of glasses. Tech writer Alex Wawro tried one of these games at a developer's conference, explaining, "I had a chance to play AR games running on a phone

The Social Trend

In the first years of virtual reality, only a few games hit the market. Game designers were unsure of the best genres for the new tech and which games would find the largest audience. By the mid-2020s, however, a strong trend in social gaming had emerged.

A social game involves playing in cooperation with several friends or strangers. There is more hide-and-seek than shooting and more casual play than real-time strategy. One of the most popular social VR games is *Gorilla Tag*, in which players embody a "monke," a legless gorilla, and use their hands to climb, jump, and walk to explore different environments.

Social VR also works with simple games, sports, and puzzles. There are VR versions of *Tetris*, a *Pinball FX VR* that allows players to set up their own pinball arcades, and *Walkabout Mini Golf*. A mysterious walk through a Tokyo subway station is the premise of *The Exit 8 VR*. The workout space is also growing an audience. In *Supernatural*, players exercise alone or in groups of two or three. They are swinging, stretching, dodging, jumping, and squatting, and the game also features guided meditation sessions.

through the glasses. I played a few rounds of DB Creations' tabletop tower defense game *Table Trenches* on an actual table, and it worked pretty well once I got the hang of using gestures to select my [defense] turrets."[13]

Eyewear for Extended Reality

The gaming industry now uses extended reality (XR) as an umbrella term for VR, AR, and mixed reality (MR) applications. Mixed reality incorporates the real and digital worlds in gameplay and usually requires a dedicated device. MR technology will rely on 3-D projection of digital elements, something like a hologram. But unlike a hologram, these elements will be interactive. Author Nicholas Sutrich describes the experience of playing a game that transforms living room walls into a vibrant town community. He writes, "In *Wall Town Wonders*, you'll be managing a tiny village that resides on the walls of your room. You'll . . . be directly controlling characters flying planes, riding on the back of miniature (yet giant) lizards, and even combing through mines to dig up ore and other resources."[14] Gameplay focuses on exploration, resource gathering and management, and construction to help the fledgling town grow and prosper.

There will be many new ways to experience such games in the future. Gaming gear is evolving to become smaller, lighter, and more comfortable. For example, in 2013 consumers could purchase Google Glass, a wearable AR device resembling eyeglasses, that projected a visible screen and responded to touch or voice commands. The wearer could even capture images and record videos. But at $1,500, Google Glass was expensive and was eventually discontinued. That did not stop Microsoft from making the HoloLens, which could project 3-D holographic images into the user's field of vision. This true MR device was an industry leader, and many corporations and institutions—including the US military—have employed it, but the even steeper price tag (roughly $3,500 for the HoloLens 2) kept it out of reach of most consumers. The HoloLens project was discontinued in 2024.

Seeing the potential for a big consumer market, though, Apple, Meta, and other companies are coming out with their own, more affordable extended reality glasses. These products boosted processing power and display capabilities. XR was also offered as a shared experience, in which users could visually connect with

Microsoft's HoloLens was an industry leader for MR devices but its steep price of $3,500 kept it out of reach of most consumers and it was discontinued in 2024.

others in the same room or across the world. Meta, a social media company, bought the Oculus virtual reality viewing system and has since produced the Meta Quest 3, an MR headset designed for more than entertainment.

Mark Zuckerberg, the CEO of Meta, had that vision when his company bought Oculus in 2014. In an interview that year, he stated, "After games, we're going to make Oculus a platform for many other experiences. Imagine enjoying a courtside seat at a game, studying in a classroom of students and teachers all over the world or consulting with a doctor face-to-face—just by putting on goggles in your home."[15]

> **"Imagine enjoying a courtside seat at a game, studying in a classroom of students and teachers all over the world or consulting with a doctor face-to-face—just by putting on goggles in your home."[15]**
>
> —Mark Zuckerberg, Meta chief executive officer

Affordable VR headsets will expand the market for these games, while popular game engines such as Unity have developed VR software development kits. The library of VR games will expand with these changes, and the same is true for AR and MR games that rely on ever more processing speed and better graphics capabilities.

In the future, specialized goggles and glasses may replace monitors, phone screens, and headsets as a viewing platform for games. They will deliver much more than hyperrealistic pictures. Eyewear will incorporate sound, special effects, and music. Beyond AR glasses will be contact lenses that perform similar functions. With a set of these lenses, the player would experience XR games without awkward gear of any kind.

Artificial intelligence will provide XR games with procedurally generated landscapes to be viewed and interacted with. XR will offer higher-resolution imagery and detailed, persistent items and characters. Music, sound effects, and speech will be integrated in this technology, creating a vivid and realistic world.

New Game Control Options

Designers are developing innovative techniques to make these interactions feel more engaging and realistic. Players will be us-

Persistent Worlds

When a digital world stays in place even when not viewed, it is known as a persistent world. Persistent virtual worlds in augmented reality remain anchored to 3-D, real-world settings that change as time passes, allowing different users to experience them anew when they log on.

Game developer Niantic currently offers Lightship, a platform for developers interested in building persistent AR worlds. The creator of a game can choose a real-world location, such as the tall "canyons" of midtown Manhattan streets, and overlay game elements that are anchored to buildings, signs, and storefronts. Gameplay might involve navigating those streets and fighting monsters while clinging to the surrounding skyscrapers. Similarly, geo-anchoring tech underlies ARKit, made by Apple. This tool places game elements at locations defined by their latitude, longitude, and altitude. A gamer using AR glasses might hike a real mountain trail, for example, to find a needed game asset at the peak.

Persistence opens some interesting possibilities in other pursuits, such as tourism. Visitors to the Colosseum in Rome might be greeted by a virtual tour guide. AR might rebuild the ancient arena as it looked two thousand years ago and even stage some digital gladiator fights for spectators.

ing voice commands, hand gestures, and skeletal tracking, which precisely traces the complex movements of the human body, to communicate, manipulate objects, and access game menus. This field, known as human–computer interaction, will combine with better computer perception to make extended reality games more immersive.

The hyperreal XR game of the future will also be enhanced through haptics, the technology of delivering physical sensations through specialized equipment. A haptic glove, for example, can deliver signals to the nerves in the hand. This allows a player to feel virtual surfaces and objects that appear on the XR screen of a headset or glasses. Finger, wrist, and thumb movements replicate the buttons and joystick functions of a console controller or the keys of a PC's keyboard.

XR games now incorporate feedback from the mind and body. A wearable device such as a bracelet can monitor a gamer's pulse and blood pressure. It also may have a neural interface that can measure psychological states, such as calmness, anxiety, focus, or excitement. Some companies see this as a way to improve mental health. "We make therapeutic virtual reality video games with live biofeedback," explains the home page of Acute XR. "Our first game, *Calm Quest*, tackles the most widespread mental health issue worldwide: anxiety disorders."[16] On the other hand, a horror game may use biofeedback to adjust the anxiety level up—not down—to increase tension and excitement.

Ultimately, gamers may be able to control progress through a game using only their thoughts. A brain control interface, which reads and responds to electrical activity in the brain, could allow gamers to think a command or movement and have it translated into action within the game. This would make many action games more accessible to disabled players who may have lost the use of their hands.

With these advances in tech, XR games of the future will overcome the physical limitations of traditional video games. Instead of consoles or PCs, games will be played on more portable platforms such as headgear or glasses. Players will not need a cable or other connectors to play the game. Their gaming space can be expanded outdoors and into the wider world. "With the use

XR games of the future will be played on more portable platforms such as headgear or glasses. Players will not need a cable or other connectors to play games.

of XR tech and wearables, gamers get to feel like the principal characters in a game," comments Hummingbirdsday on the Medium platform, "while absorbing all the action like they would in the real world."[17]

> **"With the use of XR tech and wearables, gamers get to feel like the principal characters in a game while absorbing all the action like they would in the real world."[17]**
>
> **—Hummingbirdsday, the pen name of user experience designer Dominique Wu**

Humans are social animals, and there has always been a strong drive to join or observe others in competition, whether it is the Olympic Games or *Call of Duty*. XR games of all kinds are offering unique social experiences. Players can form a small group of friends, or an online community, for a cooperative hide-and seek, an exciting tank battle, or a showdown with a crowd of zombies. Multiplayer gaming has been popular since the 1990s, and social gaming will take this trend even further, relying on the new capabilities of the online, virtual computing space known as the cloud to host larger social gaming events.

Cloud Gaming and the Metaverse

First developed in the 1990s, massively multiplayer online games (MMOs) have taken over the gaming world. The growing number of platforms and storage space on the internet made it possible. Massive communities of dedicated players now log on to enjoy battle royales in *World of Warcraft* and *Fortnite*. Others build their own imaginary worlds in *Roblox* or *Minecraft*. The alternate reality of online communities that sprang up around these games is often called a metaverse—a combination of *meta*, meaning "transcending," and *universe*. The metaverse is not a single, online virtual world; there are multiple metaverses for each community. Participants assume new identities in a metaverse and represent themselves with names and avatars—virtual characters—they design. Each player can assume a distinct identity in many different metaverses.

MMOs and metaverses live in the cloud, a virtual space defined by the storage and processing capacity of several networked remote servers. Even though most people speak of "the" cloud, there are many separate clouds, each composed of its own servers supporting an online activity. For gaming, a cloud stores each game's maps and NPCs and allows players to log on to participate. Faster connection speeds and processing power of personal computers have made all the difference in the MMO experience. The price of admission to these worlds was the expense of hardware capable of handling online games. In the years to come, this aspect of cloud gaming will likely change.

The Streams to Come

Because many games can now be played in the cloud, experts predict that video games will turn to streaming technology and the subscription model to reach the largest audience. This technology was first used by services such as Netflix to deliver movies and television shows to customers who pay a monthly fee to join. In the 2020s video games began appearing on streaming platforms.

Netflix offered the street racer game *Grand Theft Auto* and a party game, *Boggle Party*, as well as original games designed exclusively for the platform. It has since added more than one hundred mobile titles and partnered with gaming companies to offer companion games to streaming shows built on franchise properties. For example, Netflix has announced it has partnered with Ubisoft to host some unique *Assassin's Creed* titles in concert with a new series based in that video game world.

Subscriptions and streaming platforms are changing the gaming experience for some players. Netflix's subscribers can log on and play a game by scanning a QR code with a mobile phone and

Massively multiplayer online games have taken over the gaming world. Huge communities of dedicated players now log on to enjoy battle royales in World of Warcraft *(pictured) and* Fortnite.

then using the phone as a game controller. Amazon's Luna platform works in the same manner. The games on these platforms are casual or indie mobile games, not memory-intensive titles that demand fast computer processors to function properly.

Current gaming marketplaces like Steam require video game purchasers to download games onto a computer or device to play. Steam also offers Remote Play, allowing a player to stream games from a PC to devices such as a laptop, a television, or a mobile phone. Nvidia and Microsoft also have game-streaming platforms, which are making dedicated consoles obsolete.

In 2020 Gareth Wilson, a creative director at Traveller's Tales, predicted, "Streaming technology will become mainstream in the next 10 years. As network infrastructure catches up, it'll be commonplace to buy a game and immediately start playing it via streaming."[18] While Netflix, Amazon, and other streaming services have made this happen with smaller, simpler titles, future advances in the graphics processing capabilities of servers and low-lag, high-speed internet could allow the most demanding top-tier games to be accessed without a console or computer.

"As network infrastructure catches up, it'll be commonplace to buy a game and immediately start playing it via streaming."[18]

—Gareth Wilson, creative director at Traveller's Tales

Developers of all sizes will benefit from streaming. There will be no need to program a game for different platforms and hardware because a single cloud provider such as Netflix, Amazon, or Google will host the game. Moving from consoles and PCs to the cloud will also allow independents to try out new game modes and designs. A huge investment of time and money into a single game will not be necessary. Through cloud subscription gaming, developers will earn a steady stream of money, and seek to profit from content that is new and unfamiliar. Entertainment might evolve to merge video game narratives with the stories offered in streaming shows. Simplestream, a website that deals with the streaming industry, predicts that "as technology advances, we can expect more cross-platform experiences where the narrative of a game continues on a streaming platform, or vice versa."[19] The goal is

Developers of all sizes will benefit from streaming. There will be no need to program a game for different platforms because a single cloud provider such as Netflix can host the game.

to allow viewers and players to be more active participants in an immersive crossover experience.

AI and the Cloud

To effect many of these changes in video game content and access, creators will develop these games in partnership with artificial intelligence. AI will enhance cloud gaming and MMOs. For example, this technology will transform the role of non-player characters. "By leveraging generative AI models," explains Eric Duan on the Naavik website, "NPCs gain depth and dynamism that enable lifelike personalities and interactions—imagine an NPC that remembers past decisions, learns over time, and has its own goals and motivations."[20] In this way the player has much more effect on the progress of the game, becoming a partner rather than a passive consumer. And online hosted games might have the server capacity to allow the AI to operate efficiently, a problem that downloaded games will find a challenge to overcome.

But deploying AI in cloud gaming still requires a tremendous amount of data processing, and servers may be strained by

Play-to-Earn Gaming

Cloud gaming and metaverses allow individuals to own digital assets. In the play-to-earn (P2E) gaming model, users create, trade, and sell these assets either in-game or in a larger platform such as the Vorto Network or a metaverse community. The P2E model will also become a feature of Web3 game arcades. To persuade casual players to keep playing, these sites will offer cryptocurrency or digital tokens as rewards for reaching achievements within the game. Recipients can store these assets and crypto in a secure digital wallet. They will also be able to port their avatar and their assets from one game to the next.

There will be various ways to earn in this model. Players might acquire tradable assets by winning a battle royale, owning a stretch of land or construction in a metaverse, or making a contribution to a game's landscape, levels, weapons, or character design. Video games will not just be for fun and entertainment. They will create a lucrative career and an important sector of the economy. And they will give players a greater role in shaping a game environment.

multiple users. Iflexion, an AI consultant for game publishers, warns, "Adopting AI in gaming entails significant expenses, including hardware investments, commercial software licensing, and continuous model maintenance. Additional costs arise from hiring experts capable of developing AI models." The company has some suggestions for lessening this burden in the future, such as "[using] cloud AI services with consumption-based pricing."[21] This would mean gamers paying according to how much time, bandwidth, or processing used while playing. Another possibility is increasing advertising within games.

Companies have already established their presence in the metaverse. Just as the Coke and Starbucks logos now appear in movies, corporations have also taken up metaverse spaces. Company branding may pop up in games that need revenue. Persistent ads may appear in the user interface. Some games might be interrupted for commercial breaks. And games and platforms may charge a premium for offering an ad-free space.

Assets in the Metaverse

While companies may seek new revenue streams, so, too, can gamers. In metaverse gaming, players can become entrepreneurs. In future games, valuable items—such as clothing, weapons, vehicles, or abilities—may be recovered as part of in-game loot, awarded for boss combats, or purchased from other players. Players can build a secure personal inventory of digital assets that are portable, tradable, and salable for real currency.

As more players join the metaverse, the number of players taking part in the gaming economy will grow. Among them, a market for assets will grow, allowing players to earn income from the metaverse. As this ecosystem expands, ambitious players will set up companies of their own to offer game services and tradable assets. Cloud gaming exchange will likely emerge as an entirely new class of business and employment.

> "Social experiences in game spaces lay the foundation for other online activities, such as concerts, sporting events, and other aspects of life, including work and commerce. The growing demand for community experiences is becoming a catalyst for a broader metaverse."[22]
>
> —Bain consulting firm survey

But gamers in the metaverse see it as a place where playing games and trading game assets is just one thing to do. A survey taken by the consulting company Bain, for example, found that gamers preferred taking classes in the metaverse. Most of them would also prefer to buy a vacation home in the metaverse rather than in the "real" world. The survey concluded: "Social experiences in game spaces lay the foundation for other online activities, such as concerts, sporting events, and other aspects of life, including work and commerce. The growing demand for community experiences is becoming a catalyst for a broader metaverse."[22]

New Metaverse Fun

Virtual concerts in the metaverse began in the 2020s, and the concept will grow. With improved graphics and audio technology, the game cloud will replicate the live concert experience in the home or school. The show may include holographic projections of the performers, a song list that can be rearranged by the viewer, and a menu of real-world merchandise for sale.

Incorporating gaming with live performance also holds possibilities. For example, stand-up comedians may arrange perfor-

Virtual concerts in the metaverse began in the 2020s. With improved graphics and audio technology, the game cloud will replicate the live concert experience.

mances within a space-themed MMO with more than a billion players around the world. The jokes and stories might reference the imaginary distant planet being fought over by online gamers in a cosmic battle royale.

Such collaborations demonstrate that metaverse events will bring people together. Within gaming, certain platforms are already facilitating interpersonal experiences. In-game chat subjects, for example, can wander from game strategy to the weather outside to the gamer's upcoming vacation. Sharing thoughts and experiences can even help make isolated individuals feel connected to a reliable group of friends who are always willing to meet online.

New Tech for the Metaverse

These worlds will be available via AR glasses and other post-screen interfaces (meaning interfaces that are not traditional computer monitors) that will be made possible via spatial computing, a new technology of the 2020s. "Spatial computing is about post-screen computing interfaces that are increasingly simple and react to speech and gestures," explains Mike Bechtel, chief futurist at Deloitte Consulting. "We're going to realize in about five years how clunky and unnatural it was to log into a rectangle for everything."[23] Using glasses or other portable devices will allow for virtual simulations to seem more natural and interactive than they would on a traditional monitor.

Mobile technology goes through a new generation of upgraded capacities every few years. The 6G generation of phones will roll out in the 2030s. They will offer detail-rich gaming platforms for citizens of the metaverse, with links to AR glasses, neural interfaces, and haptic devices. Along with better graphics and faster processors, developers will have a better tool kit to create niche games focused on very specific player markets.

The Future of Esports

Esports began with the Intergalactic *Spacewar!* Olympics at Stanford University in 1972. First prize was a year's subscription to *Rolling Stone* magazine. Since then, esports have become a very big business, with the top players earning millions in prize money as well as sponsorship fees.

Some believe that future esports will follow the path of traditional sports. Schools will offer competitive gaming, and some parents will enroll their kids in an esport program. South Kent School in Connecticut, and others, have started esports programs that cost less than traditional sports and offer training and participation from home.

Esports are big in Korea, Malaysia, Japan, and all over Europe. In 2022 the Commonwealth Games, held in the United Kingdom every four years, included esports competitions. Malaysian players won the events and took home three gold medals. In the same year, gamers met at the Asian Games for a tournament that featured competitions in *League of Legends*, *Dota 2*, and *EA Sports FIFA*. Writer Amanda Holiday reports that "the International Olympic Committee (IOC) recently gave the go-ahead for dedicated esports Games—separate from traditional Olympics—to start in Riyadh in 2027." This may lead to esports at the 2028 Summer Olympic Games, which will be held in Los Angeles.

Amanda Holiday, "Esports at the Olympics: Could 2028 Be Their Breakthrough Moment?," Dolphins Talk, September 19, 2025. https://dolphinstalk.com.

Some mobile industry leaders believe that 6G tech will bring many of the metaverse visions to life, making fully possible gaming economies, holographic gaming, and other innovations. "We have already laid the connectivity foundation with 5G, but as our networks become more powerful in the next decade so will the power of the metaverse," writes Nishant Batra of Nokia. "It is in the 6G era of 2030 that the full potential of the metaverse will be realized."[24] In his article Batra also describes technology of the future that would comprehend human action and intent—which would bring an entirely new set of possibilities to the gaming world.

"It is in the 6G era of 2030 that the full potential of the metaverse will be realized."[24]

—Nishant Batra, chief strategy and technology officer at Nokia

"The metaverse is coming," says Jensen Huang, CEO of Nvidia, a company that has become the biggest in the world by making chips for gaming platforms and computers. "Metaverse is not only a place to game. Future worlds will be photorealistic, obey the laws of physics, and be inhabited by human avatars and AI beings."[25] Huang and Nvidia are planning to ride the metaverse wave in the future by developing tools for building 3-D graphics in virtual worlds—the basic building block of the future metaverse.

Future Genres and Future Tech

In the early history of video games, there were only a few different game types. Players had their pick of platformers, first-person shooters, role-playing games, racing games, and puzzle games. Everyone had their favorite genre. Developers created new games in these genres because the games were familiar to the market and they sold well.

In the 1990s developers moved away from writing unique code for each game and began adopting game engines that provided similar architecture and mechanics for a variety of distinct narratives. The 1998 *Unreal Engine*, for instance, served as the template for several first-person shooters such as *The Wheel of Time* and *Harry Potter and the Sorcerer's Stone*. The engine could be licensed, and designers could therefore avoid coding from scratch. This made the whole process less expensive but kept genre options limited.

In the 2010s computer processing power improved, as did connection speeds used for online games. This made it possible for developers to build more complex games that combined traditional genres. A role-playing game, for example, could be fused with a first-person shooter. The result was an action role-playing game, a hybrid game genre seen in top-selling games such as *Diablo* or *Elden Ring*.

Many of these game genres will endure in the future, but the way players experience them may change. One important trend that is now arriving in all these classic genres is personalization. "Imagine a role-playing game (RPG) that adapts its

In the 2010s developers began to combine traditional genres. The top-selling Diablo *was one of the first hybrid games, fusing role-playing with the first-person shooter genre.*

storyline based on your choices or even learns from your playing style!" explains an Oreate AI blog. "Such advancements could lead to an era where every player's journey is uniquely crafted—an exciting prospect indeed."[26]

> "Imagine a role-playing game (RPG) that adapts its storyline based on your choices or even learns from your playing style!"[26]
>
> —Oreate AI, an AI workspace website

By the 2020s, game genres were multiplying beyond simple combinations. The demand for innovation in games means that in the future, developers will strive to come up with some new story, setting, or gameplay with each new release. Some of these experiments will turn into popular genres, each with a loyal audience of gamers who have found a new style to their liking.

Sandbox Games

Sandbox games arrived in the 1980s with games like *Elite*, *SimCity*, *Zoo Tycoon*, and *Wasteland*. These games offer expansive worlds to explore while also giving players the freedom to build, modify, and influence the storyline. Like a child's sandbox, they encourage open-ended creativity and experimentation. Many also support social interaction, allowing multiple players to share and shape the same world at the same time.

Inspired by LEGO blocks, *Minecraft* became a global sandbox phenomenon after its launch in 2009. Players created their own blocky homes and cities. They invented quests, mini-games, and environments. There were as many different games in the *Minecraft* world as there were players, and the upgrades and enhancements available on the platform brought a flood of revenue to Microsoft, which bought the game from the original developer, Mojang Studios.

Building and socializing in a world is the goal of some sandbox games, but most feature open-ended storylines so that players are not forced to move from one setting to the next and engage with opponents in a predetermined manner. Modern titles in the genre give more creative control to the player. In the 2026 sandbox game *Hytale*, players can build structures, shape terrain, and even alter the specific details of in-world assets without having to know difficult coding. Simon Collins-Laflamme, the game's founder, explained to a reporter, "For the

Brains and Games

As of 2026 neural link games were still just a futuristic concept. But the neural link itself is very real, with the first operating in a human in early 2024. With an implanted coin-sized device, a neural link can read neurons with a set of 1,024 tiny electrodes that resemble threads. The electrodes work as a feedback device, recording the activity of individual neurons in the brain and stimulating those that control specific activity, such as the movement of fingers or limbs. They are currently adapted to some prosthetic limbs.

Elon Musk, chief executive officer of Neuralink, claims that the first neural link product, Telepathy, will allow the user to control a mobile phone or a computer. Noland Arbaugh, who was paralyzed in a swimming accident, became the first human to receive a Telepathy implant. With the device, Arbaugh found that he could move a cursor on a monitor to play chess, as well as *Mario Kart* and the real-time strategy game *Civilization VI*.

Eventually, the neural link may be available to all consumers. This may lead to hands-off control of any video game.

first time, artists and game designers can take full ownership of world generation. . . . This is a fundamental shift away from a world shaped almost solely by programmers."[27]

Decentralized Games

Experts predict that future sandbox games will combine with other genres such as survival, horror, racing, sports, and puzzle games. Users will create maps, design items, and set up the quests or events in which players will compete. A single game will be available across multiple platforms, from PC to console to mobile.

Other changes will be driven by innovative uses of the internet. Some sandbox games, for example, may adopt the structure of a decentralized autonomous organization (DAO). This means building the game and then turning it over to players, who then decide on the rules, the gameplay, and the visual style. Blockchain technology allows a secure way to protect assets and set up unbreakable contracts among the gamers. This digital record

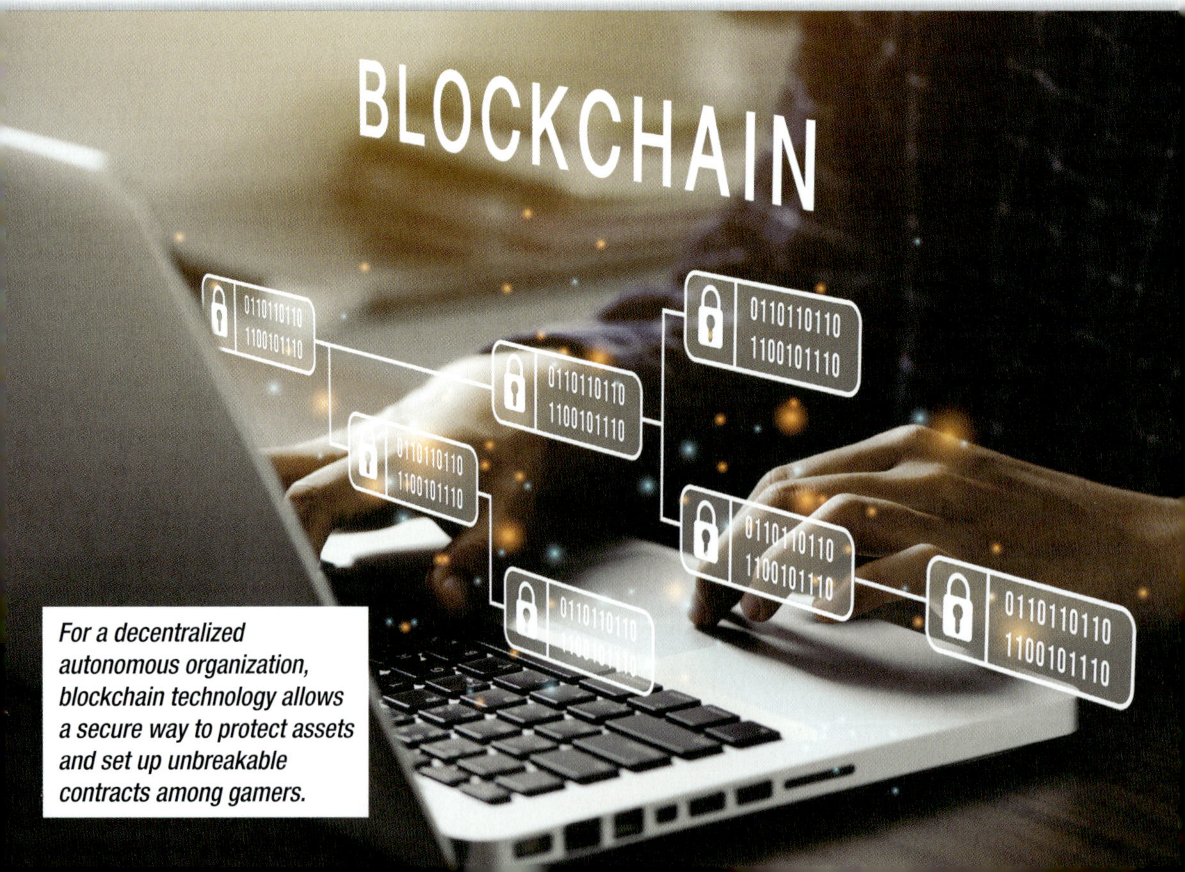

For a decentralized autonomous organization, blockchain technology allows a secure way to protect assets and set up unbreakable contracts among gamers.

secures data in encrypted blocks. Nobody can change or delete the data without others in the DAO agreeing.

Some games will be set up as a business, in which players earn revenue through innovative design, game achievements, and the sale of in-game merchandise. Decentralized games will not be limited to the sandbox genre. In theory, any kind of game can offer a DAO structure, putting the players in control. "Blockchain games present opportunities for users to buy or win digital assets," explains the website Chainalysis. "Gamers can keep or sell these assets on decentralized marketplaces in exchange for fiat [real] money. Blockchain gaming can put gamers in control of their own data and assets, allowing them to move them from one platform or game to another as it suits them."[28]

Play to Survive

Building on sandbox open worlds, the survival genre became popular in the 2020s, and many gamers are now thoroughly hooked on these stories about just staying alive. In a survival game, players manage resources and their own health to overcome a dire, life-threatening situation, such as a shipwreck in shark-infested waters, a climb up a rugged mountain peak, or a zombie apocalypse. In *The Forest*, gamers have cannibal mutants to deal with, while in *Subnautica* there is a whole host of dangerous predators waiting under the ocean's surface. Skillful players harvest resources to build better equipment, establish bases, and take on stronger opponents.

New technology poses interesting possibilities for the survival genre in the future. Augmented reality may allow players to see the world they are trying to survive in through goggles in 3-D, while in mixed reality the sharks, volcanoes, and zombies appear right in front of the player, on top of the real world and scarily realistic.

Game studios are also experimenting with the genre to create environments that react intelligently to the player's own moves and style. A future generative AI survival game may also simply serve as a template, with the player instructing the game on the time and place, as well as the mechanics of securing food, shelter, tools, and weapons.

Social Games

Another genre that gained a following in the 2020s is the social deduction game. Gameplay is not about finding treasure, battling bosses, or racing to the finish line. Instead, social deduction games challenge members of a group to complete a shared goal or series of tasks while trying to determine who among them is an ally and who is secretly working against the group. Some players may be trying to sabotage the mission; others might be working on private objectives the game has provided. Interaction with the other players and the ability to separate truth from deception are necessary to succeed.

Games without competition are another trend that attracts groups. Some simulations—or sims—allow players to construct an alternate life in a new environment and set their own pace and objectives. There are farming sims, city-building sims, and vehicle sims that allow players to re-create real-world experiences. *SpaceChem* is a puzzle-building sim for PCs in which players creatively design circuits through which molecules can flow and bond.

Sim games in the future will be more specialized and more realistic. This game genre can be applied to any line of work or play: running a car factory, playing in a rock band, or managing a squad of top-level martial arts combatants. Simulation templates allow players to transform virtually any setting or activity into a complex system of building, management, and social interaction. Cooperative sims will allow players to work together or in competition to build the biggest and best version of whatever real-life process, event, or pursuit interests them.

Advanced technology will also give rise to new sim experiences. A mixed reality version of the genre, for example, may allow a fascinating new *Zoo Tycoon*. Instead of raising a zoo on a screen, the player may be able to construct one on a tabletop, placing the zebras, tigers, wild horse plains, and dolphin tanks

The Future of Rhythm Games

It seemed as if rhythm games could not go far after *Dance Dance Revolution*. But video game developers are resourceful when it comes to improving on something outdated. The concept of the *Dance Dance Revolution* arcade game was simple: players danced on a mat-style controller in time to the music. In the 2020s the anime-style *Unbeatable* refreshed the idea for consoles, leading gamers through the story of Beat, a singer with a band on the run, performing in a place where music is against the law. In this new game, players use two controller buttons to try to perform actions in time with a soundtrack.

Rhythm games are quicky moving into virtual reality and augmented reality spaces. *Beatable* is a rhythm virtual reality game that tracks the hands and turns the tabletop, or any surface, into a musical instrument. It is at the leading edge of mixed reality games that combine the real and digital worlds. Then there is *Rhythm Doctor*, in which the gamer plays a physician. To heal a patient with heart trouble, steady hands are prescribed. Each patient has a unique heartbeat, based on a different musical meter, and success involves mastering fast beats and tricky rhythm patterns.

on the corners of the table and the concessions in the middle. Virtual reality is one example of a new tech that created a new kind of game. There will be many more in the future as computer research improves the realism of worlds built by video gamers.

Games and Social Media Collide

If there is one activity that competes with video games for time and attention, it is social media. By 2026 Facebook alone had gathered more than 3 billion active users. Instagram, TikTok, and WhatsApp also serve huge communities around the world. These platforms attract and hold users with a variety of strategies that come from video games. An engagement loop, for example, is a game mechanic or activity that rewards players and keeps them logged on to the game. User engagement has also become a key metric for social media platforms that use endless content to keep viewers scrolling.

Games are becoming a form of social media. Multiplayer games are a way for members of a big community to have some fun together and for gamers to get out of their personal bubbles and interact. *World of Warcraft* and *Roblox* are games that make socializing a key element of the experience. *Fortnite*, though it started out as a battle royale first-person shooter game, has evolved into a big global party of dedicated players, who enjoy some unique features such as live in-game concerts.

Roblox leads the trend of integrating the social side into game design. Between building block towers, fighting deathmatches, and crawling through dungeons, users will post their vacation photos and reach out to long-lost friends. A newsfeed might be available, and the game will push out ads tailored to the player's interests and taste. It is possible that Facebook and other social sites will turn themselves into massive games, just to keep long-time users interested.

New technology promises to gamify social media. In her LinkedIn blog, Simran Jaiswal suggests a 3-D future: "Holographic social media, powered by breakthroughs in light-field displays, augmented reality (AR) headsets, and holographic projectors, is turning digital interactions into immersive, three-dimensional experiences."[29]

Holographic Games

Holograms are becoming a key element of XR gaming. "Holographic technology opens doors for innovative game mechanics," reports the entertainment consulting agency Ortmor. "Imagine dodging fireballs that appear to whiz past you or feeling the resistance of a virtual object as you interact with it. This level of interactivity promises to blur the lines between the real and virtual worlds."[30]

> **"Imagine dodging fireballs that appear to whiz past you or feeling the resistance of a virtual object as you interact with it."[30]**
>
> —Ortmor, an entertainment consulting agency

Some games of the future will deploy a holograph system that can project a 3-D image into a room, onto a tabletop, or within an outdoor environment. A role-playing game may become a realistic experience through which players can move, fight, and explore a dungeon, spaceport, or any other environment. Nonplayer characters and level bosses appear full-sized and interac-

Some games of the future will deploy a holograph system that can project a 3-D image into a room, onto a tabletop, or within an outdoor environment.

tive. Some AR games might rely on the layout of a real house or other space overlaid with gameplay elements.

Holographic games will need holographic projectors. But they will allow players to control the game's functions with their own gestures. A hand wave may start a magic spell, which the player retrieved with a head nod at one of the game's gear menus. Players may be able to switch levels or scroll through costumes by blinking their eyes.

"The eSports streaming stage is all set for interactive, immersive, and high-definition streaming experiences."[31]

—Richi Milan, content marketer at Muvi

Holographic projection will also change esports and the streaming of gamer events. Fans of top gamers will be able to follow their battles as projections onto any wall or into any 3-D space. Computer processing, internet capacity, and evolving technology will bring these changes to esports streaming. "With advances in video resolution, 5G technology, AI, ML (machine learning), and VR/AR," writes Richi Milan on Muvi, "the eSports streaming stage is all set for interactive, immersive, and high-definition streaming experiences."[31]

Neural Link Games

Beyond these updates to current gaming technology, another innovation promises amazing changes in many different genres. Brain implants called neural links have important applications in the gaming world. Currently, neural links are allowing physically disabled individuals to play games through an interface between the brain and a computer. In the future, neural links might be widespread. They could be used in gaming to measure emotions such as fear, relaxation, excitement, or boredom and modify the parameters of a game. A neural link game, for example, might reward players for their intensity or focus. A player who can stay calm throughout a turbulent scene may be able to unlock new levels or gain points.

Games could also rely on these interfaces to adjust themselves to the player's mental state. If a gamer gets frustrated, the game may make itself easier. A state of boredom in the gamer may trigger more exciting levels or an interesting puzzle challenge. A feedback system could serve as the game controller. Players would set aside any devices and simply move through the game, and take actions inside the game, with their thoughts.

Neural link gaming can also help people who suffer from psychological disorders. A combat vet with post-traumatic stress disorder, for example, might be able to ease symptoms with a feedback game that rewards states of calm or concentration.

Integrating a neural link into games is one way for developers to move their industry forward and stay on the cutting edge of fun. Not everyone will want their thoughts and emotions read by a game, of course. In the future of game development, there will be popular hits and critical misses, successes and failures. The most important facet of video games will remain the drive to create something new and surprising in the attempt to capture a slice of the biggest entertainment business of all.

SOURCE NOTES

Introduction: Strange New Games

1. Contrary Research, "Video Games and Engineering Virtual Worlds," December 13, 2023. https://research.contrary.com.
2. Tencent Cloud, "What Is the Future Application Prospect of Speech Recognition in Virtual Reality and Augmented Reality?," August 6, 2025. www.tencentcloud.com.
3. Inworld, "NPCs, Past, Present and Future." https://inworld.ai.

Chapter One: The Backstory

4. Matthew Loh and Kwan Wei Kevin Tan, "Mark Zuckerberg May Do a Twitch Stream of Himself Gaming," Business Insider, October 10, 2024. www.businessinsider.com.
5. Matthew Ball, "The Tremendous Yet Troubled State of Gaming in 2024," Matthew Ball personal website, January 23, 2024. www.matthewball.com.

Chapter Two: The Influence of AI

6. Globant, "AI in Gaming," 2026. www.globant.com.
7. Quoted in Cam Shea, "The Games Industry on What Gaming Might Be like in 2030," IGN, June 24, 2020. www.ign.com.
8. Quoted in Allan Stafford, "The Future of AI in Gaming: What's Here and What's Next," *Forbes*, August 5, 2025. www.forbes.com.
9. Seele, "Build Any Game with AI: Just Chat," 2026. www.seeles.ai.
10. Austin Gallagher, "A Critical Look at an Uncritical Article: Responding to the Unnerving Future of A.I.-Fueled Video Games," Medium, July 29, 2025. https://austingallag.medium.com.
11. Quoted in Jonathan Bloom, "AI Has Joined the Game: How Artificial Intelligence Is Changing the Video Game Industry," NBC Bay Area, April 29, 2025. www.nbcbayarea.com.

Chapter Three: Entering Extended Reality

12. Quoted in Bruce Sterling, "Augmented Reality: 'The Ultimate Display' by Ivan Sutherland," *Wired*, September 28, 2009. www.wired.com.
13. Alex Wawro, "I Just Saw the Future Through AR Glasses, and It Looks Wild," Tom's Guide, March 30, 2024. www.tomsguide.com.
14. Nicholas Sutrich, "One Year Later, Mixed Reality Games Are Booming," Android Central, November 21, 2024. www.androidcentral.com.
15. Quoted in Kyle Russell, "Mark Zuckerberg: Here's Why I Just Spent $2 Billion on a Virtual Reality Company," Business Insider, March 25, 2014. www.businessinsider.com.
16. Acute XR, "Our Services," 2025. https://acutexr.com.
17. Hummingbirdsday, "XR in Games," Medium, October 25, 2019. https://hummingbirdsday.medium.com.

Chapter Four: Cloud Gaming and the Metaverse

18. Quoted in Shea, "The Games Industry on What Gaming Might Be like in 2030."
19. John Burrnett, "Are Video Games Shaping the Future of Streaming Content?," Simplestream, June 3, 2024. www.simplestream.com.
20. Eric Duan, "AI NPCs: The Future of Game Characters," Naavik, December 1, 2024. https://naavik.co.
21. Maria Bura, "AI in Video Games: Applications, Challenges & Industry Examples," Iflexion, August 31, 2025. www.iflexion.com.
22. Anders Christofferson et al., "Young Gamers and the Metaverse: How the Rules of Success Are Changing," Bain & Company, 2026. www.bain.com.
23. Quoted in Esther Shein, "Top Metaverse Platforms in 2026, Rise of Spatial Computing," TechTarget, December 12, 2025. www.techtarget.com.
24. Nishant Batra, "6G: The Network Behind the Complete Metaverse Experience," Nokia, www.nokia.com.

25. Quoted in Bernard Marr, "The 10 Best Metaverse Quotes Everyone Should Read," *Forbes*, August 15, 2022. www.forbes.com.

Chapter Five: Future Genres and Future Tech

26. Oreate AI, "Exploring the Future of Mobile Game Genres." www.oreateai.com.
27. Quoted in Dustin Bailey, "This New Approach to Gaming Will Redefine the Block Game Genre," GamesRadar+, January 5, 2026. www.gamesradar.com.
28. Chainalysis, "What Is Blockchain Gaming?," November 15, 2023. www.chainalysis.com.
29. Simran Jaiswal, "Beyond Screens: The Dawn of Holographic Social Media," LinkedIn, August 10, 2025. www.linkedin.com.
30. Ortmor Agency, "Revolutionizing Entertainment: The Futuristic Frontier of Holographic Gaming," 2026. www.ortmoragency.com.
31. Richi Milan, "The eSports Streaming Explosion: Tap Into the Future of Online Game Streaming," Muvi, September 2, 2024. www.muvi.com.

FOR FURTHER RESEARCH

Books

Matthew Ball, *The Metaverse: Building the Spatial Internet*. Liveright, 2024.

Pippin Barr, *The Stuff Games Are Made Of*. MIT Press, 2023.

Lucy Chow, *Changing the Game: Discover How Esports and Gaming Are Redefining Business, Careers, Education, and the Future.* River Grove, 2022.

Dynamo Limited, *Level Up 2026: An AFK Book.* Scholastic, 2025.

Tim Fields, *Game Development 2042: The Future of Game Design, Development and Publishing*. CRC, 2023.

Internet Sources

Christopher Dring, "Seven Reasons to Be Hopeful About the Video Games Industry," GamesIndustry.biz, February 2, 2024. www.gamesindustry.biz.

Ernst & Young, "What's Possible for the Gaming Industry in the Next Dimension?" www.ey.com.

David Lumb, "I Saw the AI Future of Video Games: It Starts with a Character Hopping over a Box," CNET, March 30, 2025. www.cnet.com.

Perforce, "2025 State of Game Technology," 2026. www.perforce.com.

Cedric Schulte, "Gaming Trends We Think Will Die Out (or Seriously Change) in 2026," GamesHub, January 15, 2026. www.gameshub.com.

Cam Shea, "The Games Industry on What Gaming Might Be Like in 2030," IGN, June 24, 2020. www.ign.com.

Alan Stafford, "The Future of AI in Gaming: What's Here and What's Next," *Forbes*, August 5, 2025. www.forbes.com.

Websites

Game Developer

www.gamedeveloper.com

This news site covers video game releases, news about video game companies, and interviews with game developers. The site also offers tips to aspiring game creators and features podcasts that cover everything from video game trends and a look at the future of the industry to conversations among gamers about their favorite video games.

GamesIndustry.biz

www.gamesindustry.biz

This is an informative website on the video game industry, with an Academy page covering such topics of the future as machine learning in games and the merging of games and entertainment. There are also interesting articles by a variety of experts and industry leaders on the psychology of gaming, the creative future of the medium, and working in the video game industry.

IGN

www.ign.com/news

The news section of this big gaming information and review platform is an ideal place to catch up on new gaming trends and breakthroughs in gaming technology. Articles on movie and television tie-ins keep readers up on the merging of video games with other entertainment media.

Kotaku

https://kotaku.com

Kotaku is a popular gaming review website offering tips and advice on mastering the top games, but readers should be aware of spoilers in the articles that will take some of the suspense out of new games they want to try. The editors also do not shy away from presenting games that disappoint players, game-in-development disasters, malicious modders, and critical failures.

INDEX

Note: Boldface page numbers indicate illustrations.

PICTURE CREDITS

Cover: ZIIINVN/iStock

6: DC Studio/Shutterstock
9: Photology1971/Shutterstock
12: Colin Temple/Shutterstock
16: Yalcin Sonat/Shutterstock
19: Domenico Fornas/Shutterstock
21: Tupungato/Shutterstock
25: QINQIE99/Shutterstock
29: Deliris/Shutterstock
31: khoamartin/Shutterstock
34: PeopleImages/Shutterstock
37: Stas Malyarevsky/Shutterstock
39: Miguel Lagoa/Shutterstock
42: Creativa Images/Shutterstock
46: Trismegist san/Shutterstock
48: Khanchit Khirisutchalual/iStock
53: Frame Stock Footage/Shutterstock

ABOUT THE AUTHOR

An editor, teacher, web designer, and book author, Tom Streissguth has written more than one hundred books for young readers, covering subjects such as history, geography, current events, and media. The first novella in his ten-part fiction series, *Heroes in the Dark*, was published in April 2026. In 2017 he founded The Archive of American Journalism to publish the little-known, hard-to-find writings of major American writers such as H.L. Mencken, Nellie Bly, Stephen Crane, and Ray Stannard Baker. More than ten thousand of these pieces are now available on the company's website, and ten books of articles have been published under The Archive's imprint.